SIMPLE SCENES

How To Write Your Memoir Like A Stage Play

Rix Quinn

Copyright © Quinn Publications 2025

All rights reserved. No part of this book may be reproduced or transmitted in any form or by any means without written permission from the author.

Contents

Dedication ....
Contents iii
Dedication i
About the Author ii
Preface 1
Introduction 4
Secret 1 Study the History of Newspaper and Magazine Simple Scenes 7
Secret 2 Think of Simple Solutions 9
Secret 3 Combine Simple Scenes with Flash Fiction's Format 14
Secret 4 Building a Simple Scene Sentence-by-Sentence 17
Secret 5 How I Stumbled into the Simple Scene Idea 22
Secret 6 Combine Critical Components of a Simple Scene 25
Secret 7 Fear Is the Single Most Powerful Motivator 27
Secret 8 Formulate Great Questions: the Key to Memorable Simple Scenes 31
Secret 9 Alternative: Turn a Story Upside Down 34
Secret 10 Another Alternative Approach: the Twist 36
Secret 11 The Declare-Prepare Technique, and "Eye Breaks" 38
Secret 12 41
12 Big Advantages of Simple Scene Writing 41
Secret 13 One Single Specialty = Fame and Memorability 43
Secret 14 The Horrible Downside to Competition 45
Secret 15 Writing Simple Scenes for a Competitive Market 50

Secret 16 The Micro-Niche Approach to Simple Scenes............. 52

Secret 17 Gather Information on Flash Fiction Techniques 56

Secret 18 Prepare to Create the Perfect Title or Heading............. 58

Secret 19 Your First Sentence Is the Most Important One........... 64

Secret 20 You Don't Like My Favorite Sentences? Then Try These! 67

Secret 21 What's the Best Way to Conclude a Simple Scene?..... 74

Secret 22 Additional Uses for the Simple Scene............................ 78

Secret 23 More Types of Simple Scenes.. 82

Secret 24 Use the Simple Scenes Approach for Personal Interviews 86

Secret 25 How a Simple Scene Tackles School Essays and Reports 89

Secret 26 Simple Scenes for Speech Introductions and Reference Letters.. 94

Secret 27 A Simple Scene for Obituaries, Tributes, and Funeral Speeches.. 98

Secret 28 Other Questions about Simple Scenes 103

Secret 29 When You are Ready to Start Typing........................... 108

Dedication

This book is dedicated with love to my wife Erica, daughter and son-in-law Katie and Tyler, and grandchildren Aria and William.

I hope it will encourage them to write down their own Simple Scenes, and continue that habit for the rest of their lives.

About the Author

RIX QUINN is a lifelong Fort Worth, TX resident. He holds degrees from Texas Christian University (B.A. journalism) and California State University (M.A. with concentration in biography and anthropology).

He spent 20-plus years as an editor for the national business magazine publisher Quinn Publications, Inc. Its largest title was sold to a major publishing firm in 1989.

He then began to write national radio filler features and short stories for weekly newspapers.

He continues to write for magazines and newspapers. His weekly humor feature Quinn Minute is now self-syndicated to over 200 weekly newspapers.

He has written three books; one on developmental writing, one on successful business school graduates, and one on the Baby Boomer generation.

Preface

Don't tell me your life story. Just tell me the special, unforgettable moments that changed your life.

These moments rarely last an hour. Some last only seconds. But they can inspire you to change your schooling, your attitude, your profession, or even your entire life path.

My goal is to help you find those special moments…and then describe them in a way your readers will always remember.

Why? Because most of us can easily recall the major moments or events that changed our lives. And lots of those events were short conversations or actions.

Therefore, our goal is not a chronology, describing how we performed in high school, on our first job, etc.

Our goal is more of a memoir, generally considered to be non-fiction writing based on personal events, history, or perspective.

In this book, I want you to think of a series of separate scenes describing personal or family experiences that are entertaining, educating, or offer a useful idea. And in many cases, each story teaches a lesson.

The biggest obstacle to a personal memoir? Folks have trouble starting stories

In over 35 years as a magazine biographer, I've heard this over and over: "I've got lots of terrific stories to tell. My life story would make a good book."

But the book rarely happens because (1) the writer says, "there's plenty of time" and never starts, or (2) the words memoir or autobiography sound daunting, or (3) the person doesn't know how to begin

I define a Simple Scene as writing that combines techniques of flash fiction (short stories under 1000 words) with components of biography.

But it cannot describe your whole life. A Scene simply tells about one single event that profoundly influenced you.

I was born the son of a weekly newspaperman who became editor of an Army daily during World War II, and then a business magazine publisher. Mom was a teacher with a degree in economics. (I didn't know what an economist did until my second year of college.)

The family is chock-full of communicators.

My parents' friends were newspaper editors, columnists, sportswriters, biographers, an Associated Press correspondent, magazine publishers and editors, public relations execs, and ad agency writers.

Virtually everyone I knew wrote descriptive articles.

I wrote for the high school paper, the college literary magazine, and then graduated to find few writing jobs available. So, for a few years I wrote product copy for major department store chains. I described everything from radial tires to fishnet hosiery. (Who knew fishnet had so many uses?)

In the late 1970s I joined Dad's small trade magazine publishing company as an editor. We covered several industries. We were recognized as historians for the industries we served, and compiled memoirs of inventors, manufacturers, distributors, and retailers within those industries.

In 1989 we sold most of our work to another company. I began to write short memoirs and biographies for magazines in several industries. I also wrote a weekly humor "filler feature," which was syndicated by a national group. And I created comedy segments for a radio network.

Today, 30 years later, I still write a weekly comedy feature, and I develop short memoirs for newspapers, magazines, and book publishers.

While writing dozens of biographical sketches, I developed a story format that can be applied to personal memories and memoirs, business histories, new product creations, and even advertising and public relations.

I call each a Simple Scene . . . short, dramatic, and educational.

Introduction

A few years ago, Dad stood silently at a graveside funeral service. As he scanned the cemetery monuments nearby, one of them caught his eye.

"The marker carried the man's name, and the birth and death dates," Dad remembered. "And beneath that were three words: 'He grew peaches.'"

Dad suddenly realized that a person's life -- his specialty and his passion -- had been summed up in three words. How many of us can present our message in only a few words, or a few paragraphs?

Each Simple Scene in its purest form answers a question or solves a problem. A news story should answer who, what, where, when, why, and how.

How many of us can simplify a message so much that everybody will understand and remember it?

We spend our entire lives learning, remembering, and repeating stories. The ones that stay with us—like Goldilocks and the Three Bears or Little Red Riding Hood—inform us while imparting some sort of lesson.

Why were so many stories written? Maybe they taught a lesson, predicted the future, provided how-to details…or maybe because they were incredibly interesting!

These stories share many elements with flash fiction. (Flash fiction tells complete adventures in 1000 words or less.)

For much of my working life, I've written summaries about people, events, and products. There's a reason for this:

In an increasingly complex world, we can grow bigger by thinking smaller. Over the last century or so, advertisers have become quite skilled at presenting complete stories in 30 and 60 second formats.

We must know how to tell any story in 300 to 1000 words…or preferably less. And to be remembered, each of those episodes should solve a problem.

Great Literature in Small Packages

Here's a list of dialogs, speeches, poems, and even lyrics that reinforce one point: short, specific words remain in one's memory.

William Shakespeare's "To be or not to be" speech from Hamlet: 276 words.

Abraham Lincoln's Gettysburg Address: 272 words.

Lou Gehrig's famous retirement speech to New York Yankee fans: 273 words.

Babe Ruth's "goodbye to baseball" presentation shortly before his death in 1947: 192 words.

Edgar Allen Poe's poem "Annabel Lee": 302 words.

Jimmy Stewart's famous "lost cause" speech in the movie "Mr. Smith Goes to Washington": 179 words.

"The Road Not Taken," Robert Frost's enduring poem: 144 words.

"Old Ironsides," a poem by Oliver Wendell Holmes, Sr.: 143 words.

All four verses of The Star-Spangled Banner: 310 words.

The 300-Word Rationale

Why write every story in 300 words or less? The earliest stories (like Aesop's fables) are generally under 300 words.

The typical word length of an average full-page printed magazine ad is 100-300 words.

For stand-up comedians, typical one-line jokes are only about 20 words. Longer set-ups and storytelling jokes range from 50-100 words. Most jokes are delivered in 10-30 seconds.

Next, let's examine the "average" reader. That person reads about 250-300 words per minute.

The average American reads at the 6th grade-8th grade level. About 90% of American adults have either completed high school or have a GED certificate.

The average human attention span is only about 8 to 12 seconds.

Secret 1
Study the History of Newspaper and Magazine Simple Scenes

In this country, ultra-short features have existed since newspapers began. They were called "fillers." Here's why:

In olden days (the late 1900s) lots of short stories were created simply to fill up space. Newspapers historically set type in long "galleys," which were stories that were the width of a single newspaper column.

Sometimes, a major story would not fill up all the space allotted for it. That's when the editor started looking for very brief articles.

In the 1700s, the best-known filler author was Benjamin Franklin. He published the Pennsylvania Gazette, which reported news and local events. And he also published letters to the editor, often written under pseudonyms (including ole Ben himself).

Ben's most famous fillers were short aphorisms published in Poor Richard's Almanac. A sample: "Early to bed and early to rise makes a man healthy, wealthy, and wise."

Over the years, brief "filler" features came to mean several things. Most of these short features were "evergreen." They had no immediacy, so they could appear now, or six months or a year from now, and they would still be relevant.

These fillers could be news compilations, funny stories, historical events, food recipes, household tips, fashion advice, or question-answer columns.

I also place cartoon features in the filler category. Most of them are undated. I'm referring to both cartoon strips and single-panel cartoons.

How many cartoons do you see displayed on walls in folks' homes, or forwarded to your e-mail box?

Secret 2
Think of Simple Solutions

"Simplicity is the ultimate sophistication," said Leonardo da Vinci.

Climb aboard the Nostalgia Express train with me. Let's visit a few really old stories.

The truth is, I did not invent Simple Scenes. I just glued them together from two childhood recollections: bedtime stories and TV commercials.

Bedtime stories probably originated during the cave dwelling days. Because people didn't read or write, stories had to be easily remembered so ancient folks could repeat them to others.

Many of those simple stories became rhymes, because those were especially easy to remember.

If you were born in the 1950s, 1960s, or 1970s, you were exposed to thousands of radio and TV commercials. The vast majority were 30 or 60 seconds long. (We'll talk more about timing and frequency later.)

Did you know that about 60% of business videos are under two minutes long? Or that about 58% of viewers will stay to watch the entire video if it's under one minute?

And -- surprise! -- many of the shorter ads were presented in rhyme or song. How could I ever forget the Alka Seltzer song "Plop, plop. Fizz, fizz. Oh, what a relief it is!"

Ads were packaged to fit into a program's commercial breaks, or they were placed between shows.

Because of this, we learned to absorb information in half-minute or minute intervals.

What did these ads have in common? Both were very short. Both presented a single message.

Both ad lengths usually had only one hero. Both offered a single solution to a single problem.

Bio Magic

In ancient times (before the year 2000), consumers got the brunt of their news from newspapers, magazines, radio, and television.

If students did "research," they went to the library or consulted the family's encyclopedia. But not anymore.

Now, national news and information sites are almost infinite. If you need to find information about anything, you can simply question your computer.

There's both information and misinformation floating through the airwaves constantly.

And most of us don't have time for long, complicated explanations. We want succinct, brief explanations in about 300 words or less.

Remember 20 years ago when we watched detailed local stories on the nightly news? Now, the average local news story is about 41 seconds (about 100 words).

Popular television and radio ads still last 30 or 60 seconds. And there are a few that run only 10-15 seconds.

Have you watched any old movies lately? Some of their scenes could be several minutes long. Today's average movie scene runs 90 seconds (1.5 minutes).

A one-minute ad spot on radio or TV equals 150-200 words of script.

Today, as you define yourself to your chosen audience, we think you should attempt to present yourself, your talent, and a unique, personal, true story in about 300-500 words.

It's surprisingly simple to do…if you start with an effective story line.

Before You Start Writing

I never recommend writing a biography…only writing in episodes.

Here are two fiction books that illustrate remarkable writing style. Micro Fiction offers 50 very short stories, each under 300 words.

Flash Fiction presents 72 very short stories under 1000 words each.

Study these condensed stories which generally offer fewer characters, simpler plots, and more distinct conclusions.

These are fiction stories, but they are terrific examples of presenting any fiction or non-fiction story as a memorable scene.

Story Lines

One of my bosses insisted that I should never start a story without first crafting a powerful story line. During my school years, teachers used to describe these lines as a "thesis sentence."

My editor expected one sentence that introduced the main character, emphasized the story's path, and concluded with how the story would help the reader.

Believe me, that is one tough task. I completed that job by including the "Three Cs."

After several tries, I built story line sentences that included (a) a character, (b) a catastrophe, and (c) confession or conclusion (redemption, or changing oneself for the better).

Here are three terrific, fictional story line samples from three great childhood tales:

The Three Little Pigs: "Young hogs defeat wolf and learn that construction shortcuts can be dangerous."

Goldilocks: "Don't break into houses, or sample products without permission."

Charlotte's Web: "A brilliant spider convinces a farmer that her pig friend Wilbur is a genius who can be an asset to the farm."

What Do Readers Do With Short Messages?

As a magazine editor for 20-plus years, I stumbled onto many ways readers save valuable information.

We often visited companies that subscribed to our magazines. Most said they found our monthly articles helpful.

But what readers most frequently complimented were our fillers, those very short stories, brief sayings, or aphorisms that ran in the back of each issue.

We spent loads of time reporting on industry trends, new products, inventions, and other news. But readers constantly complimented our shortest stories. How did we know?

Because those features were either thumbtacked on readers' bulletin boards, or they were taped to refrigerators in their break rooms. Amazing.

After our magazines were sold to another company, I knew what I wanted to do in my next career. Yes…create little features with big impact.

The 'Sweet Spot'

As you know, these short messages might be called other names like a filler, mini-article, or a featurette, or trivia. I've been told that a filler is about 300-500 words, while short articles can run up to 1000 (that's longer than several syndicated newspaper columns).

But I continue to believe the "sweet spot" is about 300-500 words. That's long enough to communicate a message, and short enough to find print space almost anywhere.

Secret 3

Combine Simple Scenes with Flash Fiction's Format

I cannot find a standard length for flash fiction, but the general agreement is "under 1000 words." It's also been called many things, from micro stories to micro fiction to nano fiction to postcard fiction.

Other short fiction types are called short-short stories and sudden fiction, but those are slightly longer.

United States readers saw some early flash fiction during the 1800s, and among its most famous writers was Walt Whitman.

Two writers, Mildred I. Reid and Delmar E. Bordeaux, say the modern short-short was published in *Collier's Weekly* as early as 1925.

What's Important about Flash Fiction

1. It attempts to tell a complete story in very few words. Because of abbreviated length, it often features one main character, one scene, and one problem to solve.
2. There should be a main character, and she should move into action immediately.

3. Some writers do that by beginning their story in the middle of an action, then flash back quickly to further define the main character. Others reveal the main character through the action.

4. The best stories conclude with a dramatic change in the plot, or a dramatic change in the main character.

5. The most engaging flash fiction offers a twist or surprise ending, or a discovery. I agree, but I would add one other thing. If not a surprise finish, the story should teach a lesson.

6. Remember old cowboy movies? Nearly all began with a setting (horseback riders in a street, prairie, or ranch house). Readers must be able to visualize a person or location.

7. Write everything at 6th grade level. (Average length of words in your story should be 5 characters.)

8. Short words are reportedly the #1 predictor of readability.

9. Use simple similes, metaphors, and analogies. "The frail stranger looked like a vampire."

10. Single point of view: Main character or narrator tells the story. Use first or third person.

11. No more than two characters.

The Flash Fiction Writer Who Changed History

One of my favorite flash fiction writers is Aesop, who lived around 600 B.C. He chronicled fables from around the civilized world.

He became so famous he traveled many places to share stories with people from all segments of society.

His stories—like the one about the tortoise and the hare—gave animals human qualities. His fables pointed out people's good and bad traits and illustrated critical life lessons.

Nobody really knows what Aesop looked like, because cameras were poor in 560 B.C.

Many of these stories taught moral lessons and wisdom…and most of the fables are about 200-300 words.

Secret 4

Building a Simple Scene Sentence-by-Sentence

Is there any sort of template to build a (nearly) perfect Simple Scene story?

I think so. Just think of every story you write as a scene from a movie…even if that story is very short.

Your first few words are critical…and they should signal major trouble.

The hero attempts to solve the problem. But he fails or even makes things worse.

At some point in the story, a failure might make the situation appear hopeless.

But the hero must find a way to pull through. How does she do this? That's where your creative writing comes in.

A great example of this format is "The Three Little Pigs." And to make this story even more memorable, it contains both an ending and a valuable message.

As an alternative, think of each scene as a stage play. Many personal memoirs are written that way, as <u>a string of unrelated events </u>that reveal the main character's goals and ideals.

That means each scene should become a self-contained episode (beginning, middle, end).

Just describe a moment. Try writing the story in the present tense, just like it is happening this very minute. Limit the story – start to finish -- to 300 words or less.

Each scene has a conclusion. Or it leads to the next scene. Each one will be more memorable if it (1) solves a problem or (2) reveals how you discovered your skill – or product – is unique.

Those First Paragraphs

Within the first couple paragraphs, the villain or catastrophe should be introduced. Right up front, readers should know there's a problem, and some sort of heroic act may solve it.

If possible, stick to one main character. More than that creates confusion. (If you rewrote Humpty Dumpty, you would not want Humpty to have either a love interest or a twin brother.)

Every line of effective Simple Scenes should either provide more information, advance the story, or prepare the reader for the next paragraph.

It's also helpful if the problem gets solved in an unusual or surprising way. A good example: in Dickens' "A Christmas Carol," Scrooge's scary dream about Christmas Future convinces him to mend his ways immediately.

Nearly All Great Stories Require Conflict

"Where there is a monster, there is a miracle," Ogden Nash tells us.

Start everything with a story line. That line should include the Three C's we discussed earlier.

Can you write one sentence that (1) describes the main character, (2) introduces the conflict, and (3) tells what makes the story valuable to the reader?

How many movies have you seen over the years? How many of them involve conflict or catastrophe? 100%

Without a conflict, there is no tension. Without tension, there is no memorable story.

That conflict doesn't need to be serious. In many police shows, conflict involves chasing a dangerous criminal. I've seen lots of situation comedies where the conflict involves nothing more serious than choosing the right date to take to the prom.

If you are trying to get a job, your "conflict" might describe how you overcame an injury in sports, or how a tough math class gave you a good background for statistics.

If you've invented a new product, your conflict might involve your attempt to solve a problem. Your conflict's resolution might detail how the product works.

The conflict doesn't need to be personal. The main character might oppose another human, a force of nature, an unexpected event, or a personal problem.

Happy Conclusions are More Fulfilling

Most of us remember classic fairy tales from childhood, when the concluding words were "and they lived happily ever after."

The hero defeats the enemy or evil force. A potential disaster is avoided.

In television series of the 1950s-1970s, those temporary triumphs meant the end of that week's program. Examples: Superman, Lone Ranger, Annie Oakley.

One other thing: a happy conclusion offers intellectual fulfillment. If the main character's goals remain unfulfilled at the story's end, the episode appears incomplete.

Redemption: Even More Powerful?

There's another type of ending readers love. I call it the Redemption Resolution.

In this scenario, the hero makes a mistake. He learns a lesson when he corrects that mistake. My favorite stories of this type are "The Boy Who Cried Wolf" by Aesop and "A Christmas Carol" by Charles Dickens.

The Best Stories Come from Simple Scene Experts

A memoir is a person's collection of life memories that either reveals something about the writer's personality or shows an approach to problem-solving.

You can find many outstanding memoirs in the library today. Mark Twain, Ulysses S. Grant, and Frank McCourt (<u>Angela's Ashes</u>) all wrote terrific memoirs.

A biography often refers to an ongoing timeline. (Example: "I was born in 1960 on a cold September morning. I started kindergarten at a small elementary right near my house." Etc.)

But a memoir is not bound by such restrictions. <u>To write an effective memoir, the author can jump forward or backward on a timeline, or just dramatize a single event</u>.

To do so, she might select a theme like "teachers who influenced me." The story could start anywhere as the author describes memorable educators.

Secret 5

How I Stumbled into the Simple Scene Idea

I am a very average Baby Boomer. From my earliest years, I wrote dozens of single-page and two-page school assignments.

Remember those? We answered exciting questions like "How I spent my summer vacation" or "What person in history would you like to invite to dinner?"

I have told the following story hundreds of times…but my life suddenly changed when I accidentally won an "original playwriting" contest in eighth grade.

My idea wasn't truly original. It was an actual event in another class. As I remember, some guy stole a girl's essay and turned it in as his own. This led to a big scene, which I wrote down and then exaggerated.

My teacher was very smart, and probably expected most of the one-act plays like mine would be derived from a personal event. But she complimented my "ear for dialog." I didn't know what this meant, but I gladly accepted any praise.

High School and College

I was taught to write the "who, what, where, when, why, how" basic-facts news story on my high school newspaper. I committed that technique to memory.

As a college journalism major, I could choose the "news-editorial" specialty or the "advertising-public relations" specialty.

I went with the second one, because even then I knew I wanted to write features, biographies, or advertising communication.

I learned to write about product features in my first two jobs out of college, and the benefits customers derived from each feature.

My First Exposure to "Scene" Writing

Finally, I started writing for a small business magazine publisher who founded his company in the 1940s.

He noticed that most industry and professional magazines in those days were standard sized (8"x10").

To differentiate himself, he published his three industry magazines in a 6"x 9" size.

The smaller magazines made them stand out from the others. When they were stacked with other books, they were usually placed on top.

Other Magazines in the Late 20th Century

I soon realized that smaller equals easier to handle, carry, and display.

Reader's Digest – a digest-sized (smaller than 8"x10") magazine – became the largest periodical in the world with a circulation of 10.5 million.

Two other best-selling magazines in mid-century were TV Guide and National Geographic…also smaller sized.

Digest size is more portable. It can be stored in a closet or bathroom, and it generally has longer "shelf life." (It is often kept in the house longer, giving readers more time to see stories and ads.)

My editor also believed that small magazines should offer shorter stories. He was an expert at writing success stories, product invention articles, marketing reports, and micro-biographies in 300 words or less.

I learned from him. And I'm still learning today.

Secret 6
Combine Critical Components of a Simple Scene

How small, how simple, and how understandable can you make your message? The most powerful messages are so simple it's almost impossible to miss their meaning.

Here's a brilliant example from an English nursery rhyme: "A wise old owl sat in an oak. The more he heard, the less he spoke. The less he spoke the more he heard. Why aren't we all like that wise old bird?"

Have you noticed that much information we remember has been delivered in a problem-solution format? Both fiction and non-fiction often point out an obstacle, then propose a way to overcome it. If you cannot state a problem clearly, it's hard to propose a specific solution.

Ask a Question that Requires a Great Answer

A solid Scene begins with a story line that <u>answers a question</u>. Example: "A rabbit challenges a turtle to a race, but the turtle's persistence overcomes the rabbit's speed and inattention to detail."

Accordingly, the three components every feature must have: Three C's (character, catastrophe, conclusion).

Or, instead of a conclusion, a confession (redemption), a change for the better, or an improvement. Example: The two little piggies who built their house with cheap materials learned a lesson from their wiser brother.

I strongly believe that each paragraph should have no more than three sentences. Short lines and sentences within a story encourage readability.

The power of Declare-Prepare paragraphs

Paragraphs—as frequently as possible—should use the declare-prepare method to lead the reader from one paragraph to the next.

The first one or two sentences should declare (give information to advance the story). The last sentence should prepare the reader for the next paragraph by asking a question, or by hinting that the next paragraph will reveal even more details.

Here's a sample:

"The three little pigs left the family home one day to build their own houses. Each of them had a different idea about building material. But what components would they choose?"

Secret 7

Fear Is the Single Most Powerful Motivator

"I am an old man and have known a great many troubles, most of which never happened," said Mark Twain.

I am also an aging guy, but not quite an old man. But Mark Twain was right. Most of us spend our days fearing one thing or another.

When I was in elementary school, I was afraid I would get cut from baseball teams. In junior high, I was afraid of girls.

In high school, I feared several coaches, a few teachers, and any math course that had numbers in it. (All of them did.)

After high school, I worried about college grades, possible dates for the weekend, wearing the right shirt, and getting my hair cut properly. In my 20s these were important issues.

What's Really Important?

Some studies conclude that humans consider the game of life as one long scorecard. We mentally keep constant track of how we're doing.

Did I get the top score on the algebra test? If I didn't, what steps can I take to improve that score?

The same scenario can be prompted by a low score: I had the lowest score on the algebra test. If I fail algebra, will I get kicked out of the school's honor society? Can I take a make-up test, or get this low score erased from my record?

Tension. Tension. Tension. It's all around us.

When you write yours or another's memoir, each story must quickly spotlight and focus on the tension, and then later resolve it.

<u>Avoid All Discomfort</u>

Let's look at the activities of an average guy named Bob, and how he sidesteps pain potential each morning:

Bob views his early morning face in the bathroom mirror and prepares for his day. He soaps his beard with shaving cream, and he uses a safety razor—one that protects against skin abrasion—to alleviate his whiskers.

Next, he flosses his teeth with a product designed to prevent between-tooth cavities. Then he brushes with a whitening toothpaste to make his smile appear brighter.

He steps into the shower and lathers up with a scented deodorant soap, then washes his hair with a shampoo advertised to prevent baldness. Afterward, he applies a 24-hour deodorant, even though he'll be at work only nine hours.

After dressing, he heads for the kitchen and his morning multivitamins, formulated to help him function at peak efficiency while avoiding common maladies that slow down a 47-year-old body. He downs a steaming cup of coffee to give him energy, then gulps a bowl of cereal containing 30 or 40 healthful ingredients.

Bob's not even at work yet, but thus far he's tried to avoid facial cuts, tooth decay, body odor, creeping baldness, underarm stink, potential malnutrition, and fatigue.

Remember Twain's quote about how we avoid many troubles that probably won't happen? Bob could be the poster boy for that.

Clothes Equal Social Status

We haven't even talked about Bob's clothing for the day. Simply wearing clothes avoids the pain and embarrassment of nakedness.

But clothes can also project status. They can show that the wearer is affluent. They can indicate professions like a nurse, doctor, policeman, firefighter, or minister.

Very few clothes are sold based on utilitarian value. We don't buy a suit to keep warm. Clothes make a non-verbal statement to society.

Training and Education

How many other indirect fears do we carry around in our heads?

Let's consider education. We start worrying about our futures in high school. What subjects do I like? What do I do well? What's a job I could stand to do eight hours a day?

We take tests to determine where our skills and interests lie. Next, we select colleges or trade schools or training programs to teach us to take advantage of our special gifts.

Once we're in a career, we look for CE (continuing education) credits to help us keep current.

Education is like eating prunes. It's difficult to determine when we're getting enough, and when we've had too much.

Why We Need Insurance

Sometimes we have trouble explaining a particular problem, but we know one exists that could harm us. Those hard-to-define categories clutter our brains, and then they force us to take remedial action.

That's why one of the most important items we seek today is insurance. It not only protects us, but it also comforts our minds.

We buy home insurance to protect our property. We buy car insurance in case we're involved in an accident. And we need liability insurance to protect our savings if someone is injured on our property, or by our automobile.

We buy health insurance in case we get sick, and burial insurance so our families won't be burdened by funeral costs.

This product is miraculous, because it can help us physically if something unfortunate happens to us, and—for the present—ease our minds so we can relax and think about other things.

Bottom line: What do your readers fear? How can you describe the fear to them, and then help them lessen it?

Secret 8

Formulate Great Questions: the Key to Memorable Simple Scenes

Over 30-plus years, I made all sorts of interviewing mistakes when I tried to write micro-biographies of company founders and inventors.

Several had been interviewed so many times, they gave me "canned" answers for every question. Many of those answers sounded just like they came off the company brochure.

Finally, I decided to approach the interviews in a different way. I came up with a list of questions I suspected the interviewee had NOT been asked.

By doing so, I was able to capture new and interesting parts of their personalities previous interviewers had missed.

Here are a few sample questions I have asked. Do these help you recall pivotal events?

- ➢ Can you describe an event that changed the course of your life?
- ➢ What is a funny childhood memory your readers might enjoy?
- ➢ What is the absolute weirdest experience you ever had?
- ➢ Have you solved any problem in a funny way?
- ➢ How did you develop your skill in high school or college?

- If you could have dinner with anyone – living or dead – who would it be?
- Where have you travelled to improve your skill?
- What about being a child do you miss the most?
- Tell us about some products you remember from childhood that no longer exist.
- Predict what the world will be like in 30 years.
- Predict how your skill or product might improve that world.
- What is the happiest professional moment in your life?
- What is the biggest surprise you've ever had about your skill or product?
- What is the greatest professional comment you have heard about yourself?
- Have any famous people endorsed you? Do you have permission to use their quotes?
- Could your skill change the world for the better?

Question Catcher

Want to create even more questions to ask yourself or others? Try a "question catcher."

I keep a 3.25" x 5" pocket notebook with me all the time. (Some people just use the Notes section of a cell phone.)

Whenever I see or hear <u>anything</u> that might make a good story, I write it down.

Next to that, I write how that information might be used (college application essay, class writing assignment, diary, etc.) Later, I transfer the information to an IDEAS page of my desktop computer.

The Moth Formula

This is a nonprofit organization dedicated to storytelling. It was founded in 1997 by George Dawes Green.

It began as a gathering of friends, and it evolved into a great platform for storytelling.

They came up with the "first, last, best, worst" method. For instance, you could apply the adjectives to write about the "first (or last, best, worst) life discovery I made," or virtually any other subject. They might yield good responses.

My "Sight-and-Write" Method

This is my own silly method for asking interview questions, and it doesn't work for everyone.

I sometimes get stuck interviewing someone who volunteers very little information to my standard questions. So, I'll look around the room, spot an object, and ask a question about it.

For instance, I might try this:

"Bob, we're sitting right in front of a door. I wonder if you could tell me about someone who's opened some opportunity doors in your life?"

Or, if I notice a lamp I might ask, "What bright ideas about your business have you had lately?"

Secret 9

Alternative: Turn a Story Upside Down

Here's a personal "flip the script" story:

A close friend told me that back in high school, she became a state finalist in a future homemaker essay contest. "How did you do that?" I asked.

"I'm not sure," she recalled. "I do remember that several girls in our Homemaking classes entered, and they were astounded that my work outscored theirs.

"But maybe my essay stood out because it emphasized my mother's advice, not textbook ideas. My perceptions were different, and that caught the judges' attention."

Non-Traditional Roles, Mid-Career Changes

These are my favorite Simple Scenes to write. The main character starts in one job, then either discovers or creates another profession.

My Dad Bill was a newspaper editor before World War II, then became a business magazine editor during the profession's major growth in the 1950s.

Rodney Dangerfield worked in his family's paint and hardware store business before becoming one of the nation's most popular stand-up comedians.

Ray Kroc was a milkshake machine salesperson before joining McDonald's in his 50s.

A Powerful Positon: The Underdog

Here's a test of the underdog's powerful bite: In the following stories, who do you cheer for? The three little pigs, or the big bad wolf? Little Red Riding Hood, or the other big bad wolf?

A politician once joked that if he had "been born in a log cabin" he could have gotten more support. In recent years, several candidates presented themselves for office as underdogs or outsiders, with no connections to a political establishment.

Here are a few politicians who have successfully positioned themselves as outsiders at one time or another: Abe Lincoln, Dwight Eisenhower, Jimmy Carter, and Ronald Reagan.

Secret 10

Another Alternative Approach: The Twist

No, this is not a dance. It requires no fancy footwork. What it does require, however, is a giant leap of imagination.

We first take the reader down one predictable path. But suddenly we —or the main character—change directions.

How powerful is this? Let me paraphrase a few lines from Robert Frost's "The road not taken":

"Two roads diverged in a yellow wood, and sorry I could not travel both and be one traveler, long I stood…

"Then took the other, as just as fair, and having perhaps the better claim, because it was grassy and wanted wear…

"Two roads diverged in a wood and I—I took the one less traveled by, and that has made all the difference."

Could your life be changed by a single writing decision? Mine was. Once I embraced "the road not taken" concept, I became a different type of writer.

This poem, published in 1916—106 years ago—reveals one of the greatest short story secrets. If you must make a writing decision, choose one that the reader won't expect.

A Twist Sample

Whenever you prepare to write a story, think about the instant the problem gets solved, or the instant the mood changes. That becomes your "twist" moment. In this short story from my own life, there are two twists.

My favorite restaurant in town looked like an old-fashioned malt shop. It had a big soda fountain, and booth seating all around. They served huge double-meat hamburgers with secret sauce.

I went to the counter to pay one day, and the cashier said, "No charge, compliments of the manager." I was surprised, so I asked why. (Twist) "Oh, the manager knows you're in the seminary, and he's glad you eat here."

I apparently looked a lot like an actual seminary student, and even when I protested, they never charged me for food. Therefore, I always left a good tip.

But I couldn't beat the price of free food. However, that changed one day when I brought a date into the restaurant.

At the counter the cashier smiled and said, (Twist) "Free for you, my friend, and $3.50 for the lady's meal."

That price was still fantastic. So, every time I asked out a new girl, I took her to this cafe first. If she didn't like me, it didn't cost me much.

The first twist, of course, begins with the words "Oh, the manager knows you're in the seminary…"

So, think about the twist, and every so often…take it out for a spin.

Secret 11

The Declare-Prepare Technique, and "Eye Breaks"

Here's the technique I talked about earlier. It's absolutely, disgustingly simple. I can describe it to you in just a few basic steps.

The biggest problem with most essays, biographies, short stories, and even technical articles is that they bog down after the opening paragraph.

Therefore, I suggest that every following paragraph be three sentences or less. The reason?

People read on-screen so frequently that their eyes get exhausted. It's hard to follow line after line of gray type. (And sometimes, there are so many consecutive lines of the same length I read them twice…even with my glasses.) So, the remedy is an eye break.

The writer does this with very short paragraphs, which often finish in the middle of a typeset line. That creates white space.

In every paragraph, the first -- and even a second -- sentence can advance the story.

But the last sentence needs to build curiosity so the reader will look at the next paragraph.

Think about several acrobats in a complicated formation. Each one is linked to and supporting another. It's how the middle paragraphs should work.

I call this technique DECLARE -- PREPARE. Use it every paragraph.

Linking paragraphs creates stories. Linking stories in a book creates chapters. And so on.

Here's a sample story – my experience winning a playwriting contest -- using this technique. Note that every closing sentence in each following paragraph is a "tease" to entice the reader to continue reading.

I suspected something weird was about to happen when our speech teacher asked, "Who wants to write a play?"

She explained that the student who won the playwriting contest would get to perform it for several classes. I wanted to win, but how could I?

I had no idea. But the teacher explained to us that a good story had conflict. Suddenly I recalled that -- a few days before -- a guy got in deep trouble for stealing some girl's essay. This gave me a fantastic idea.

I immediately started writing down everything I remembered about that true classroom drama. I gave the students some fake names. But next, I needed a great ending.

So, I had the boy expelled from school for a day, but not before he begged the girl to forgive him. I won that playwriting contest, and I learned three great lessons.

It's wrong to cheat on a paper, and it's right to ask for forgiveness. But most important, I learned that the best stories contain either a great confrontation...or a bad villain.

Secret 12

11 Big Advantages of Simple Scene Writing

1. Scenes can apply to a life, an event, an invention, advice, old news, recent developments, strange occurrences, movies…virtually anything.

2. A Simple Scene can be completely single event focused. It's like a single scene in a movie. A story about Alexander Graham Bell, the telephone inventor, might concern only the moment that Bell realized a telephone call was feasible.

3. Many Scenes end with a "lesson learned" from the story. In this way, they're much like the descendants of Aesop's Fables.

4. They are usually short, because 21st century attention spans are also shorter. The ideal story is 300-500 words, about two to three minutes if read aloud. This is slightly longer than the length of an average movie scene (90 seconds).

5. Scenes can be explained in a single sentence, or "story line." Example: "The story of Three Little Pigs teaches young hogs that construction shortcuts can be dangerous."

6. A good general interest story —one offering business advice, for instance—can be sent to local television, radio, newspaper offices, and online media. It can also be pitched

to trade magazines who might want to offer the story to their industry as a public service.

7. These tiny stories are also a unique place to publicize unusual upcoming events, like the opening of a time capsule, the local appearance of a national celebrity, or oddball contests like the city's oldest dog, or most outrageous car.

8. Simple Scenes can sometimes become weekly or monthly columns. I know of one local man who because famous by developing one and two-line aphorisms that many national newspapers used.

9. A related Simple Scene is the personal interview, which can be expanded or subtracted to fill the space required. (If multiple questions are asked, the interview can be expanded to two or three articles.)

10. Human interest stories take several forms. They might be the chronology of a specific person, or they might discuss someone with a unique hobby or interest.

11. Inspirational stories are designed to uplift, and make the reader feel better. They could relate a human event, share a positive statistic (Example: "How the rabies vaccine saved 20th century lives"), or possibly inspire the reader to contribute to a charity.

Secret 13
One Single Specialty = Fame and Memorability

Here's a simple test to show your friends. But it's a way to reinforce my Dad's story about the grave marker and the short phrase that emphasized a man's life work.

Explain the test to them in the following way. Then, see if the answers I've written below are the same ones your friends provide.

"We're going to play a little game. I will give you the name of a famous person, and you tell me why you remember them."

- Goliath—Battled David in the Bible story
- Leonardo da Vinci—Painted the Mona Lisa
- Christopher Columbus—Discovered America
- Ponce de Leon—Discovered the Fountain of Youth
- Isaac Newton—Either discovered falling apples, or named gravity
- George Washington—First U.S. President
- Benjamin Franklin— Poor Richard's Almanac
- Thomas Edison—Invented the electric light bulb
- Alexander Graham Bell—Invented the telephone
- The Wright Brothers—First human flight

- Charles Lindbergh—First solo flight across the Atlantic
- Babe Ruth—Home run hitter in baseball
- Neil Armstrong—First man to land on the moon

Sure, these famous folks did other good things too. But we remember them mainly because they excelled in one area, or they distinguished themselves in one way.

Even various career fields or industries have a "hall of fame" for their specialty superstars.

In our list above, Babe Ruth won baseball fame as a home run king. But within that hall, we also recognize Abner Doubleday as the sport's inventor, and Jackie Robinson as the major leagues' first black player.

All the immortals above are recognized as the first in something, the best in something, or the only in something.

Which one are you?

Think about this. Because—when you write about yourself, or another person, or a product—your goal should be to make them the FIRST, BEST, or ONLY.

Secret 14

The Horrible Downside to Competition

Over the years, I worked on several memoirs that honored a product inventor or business innovator. I wanted to describe what made that person or product unique.

Sometimes that product was simply an improvement over what was currently available on the market. How could I write about that individual without mentioning the competition?

The only way I could find to do that was to present the product's attributes that no other competitor shared.

The answer is creating a "unique selling proposition." That's a phrase introduced in 1960 in the book *Basic Marketing* by E. Jerome McCarthy.

It simply asks: "What does my product offer that similar products do not?"

And, if you are writing a story about yourself or someone else, you could change that phrase to: "What do I offer that no one else can? What makes me unique?"

Let's say you are asked to help the inventor of a product tell the story of that item for a company newsletter. Is it possible to develop a memoir to completely sidestep competition, and leave you unchallenged in your field?

"If a first you don't succeed...quit!" Have you heard of that before? No. Usually it's "try, try again."

I guess that's logical when you struggle to pass a course or get a degree. But does it make sense when you come up against unbeatable competition?

Both good and bad things can happen in competition. I'll list the good things first, then follow up with the negative stuff. Ready? Here we go:

Competition -- the Positive

1. Competition brings out the best in you. Without someone to measure yourself against, how will you know if you've improved?

2. In the business world, competition leads to better and better products.

3. Competition leads to innovation, "building the better product."

4. Competition -- especially at the school level -- leads to recognition. The star quarterback, the top debater or speller, the outstanding math student get acclaim.

5. Competition builds character. (At least that's what I've heard.)

6. Athletic competition -- especially on the professional level -- is undeniably lucrative. It brings income to schools, colleges, communities, and to the professional athletes themselves. It is also a point of pride around which large groups congregate.

Competition -- the Negative

1. Competition began among animals as a territorial imperative. They would square off to fight over a mate or a location. Higher forms of life—including primates—found advantages in cooperative societies. Cooperation, I contend, is a better existence.

2. Competition offers two outcomes only. Either you win or you lose. And either way, you can get hurt. (Have you seen any boxing movies?)

3. Competition among little children could be counterproductive. For the less-adept young athlete, competition might even prove psychologically scarring.

4. Competition demands grand strategies and accompanying tactics. A lot of thinking goes into how to overcome an opponent.

5. Competition requires frequent countermoves. Your opponent changes plans or formations, and you must adjust for them.

6. Competition also demands extensive public relations. If your competitor comes out with a new product, it might claim your product is an inferior one. It is then up to you to disprove an accusation, which requires time and money.

7. Major elections are often decided on negative elements. "People tend to vote against someone, not for someone," a wise political analyst said. Mudslinging gets everybody dirty, and it lowers public opinion of both opponents.

8. Competitions never end. "We'll get 'em next year" is a common comment of the defeated sports team.

9. Competition costs money. Money which could be better spent for charity, research-and-development, salaries, or employee compensation.

10. Competition is mentally and physically taxing. It takes a long-term toll on its practitioners.

Shrink, Expand, Reverse, or Invent

Way, way back in the early 1960s, the auto industry manufactured long, roomy, luxurious passenger cars.

Then a remarkable print advertisement from Volkswagen turned people's perceptions upside down. On a huge page it showed a little VW Beetle in the distance. The headline said, "Think small."

In the late 1950s and early 1960s, most other car companies were thinking giant. Their cars were huge, with gigantic tail fins and powerful engines.

The brilliant ad campaign pointed out the advantages of owning this smaller car. Those included things like great gas mileage or getting into a small parking spot.

Postscript

If you believe, as I do, that competition is self-defeating:

Why go head-to-head with anybody? Why subject yourself to pain? If you don't succeed by competing...quit!

Even when writing memoirs, maybe you should create, innovate, and constantly isolate the main character and/or the product.

What can you do that's less, more, larger, smaller, a different color, a different shape, or a different price?

Secret 15

Writing Simple Scenes for a Competitive Market

Many professionals say that the secret is to find one major obvious ability that potential competitors do not have.

The second challenge is to determine how many potential clients would rank that ability as the major reason for choosing you.

Examples: a tax accountant who works for dentists only; a writer who builds short biographies for corporation chief executive officers; a golf instructor who teaches only chipping and putting.

How are you different from other people or companies?

My favorite "differentiator" is Avis, who said they tried harder because they were not the biggest.

Polaroid became the leader in instant photos competing against film, which needed to be developed.

Ben & Jerry's promoted their ice cream with different flavors and social causes.

Federal Express competed against the post office by focusing on overnight delivery.

Five Hurdles You Must Leap to do This

Unique – Your idea must be completely different, one unfamiliar to your profession or industry.

Scarce – It must not be available anywhere else. You are the source.

Newsworthy – It must be something that immediately attracts attention.

Track record – It must demonstrate some degree of success.

Narrative – It must tell a story that answers the question "What makes this valuable?"

Secret 16

The Micro-Niche Approach to Simple Scenes

An expert is not some high-powered superhuman. She is simply a person who's well versed in a subject. All of us are experts on something.

I gained experience in short writing by talking to lots of editors, asking what they wanted and, more important, what they did not want.

I learned that the smaller a field, the fewer people will be found cultivating it. Here's an idea for narrowing your focus:

Let's say you own an acting studio. So do lots of other people.

How can you separate yourself? How about focusing on one type of show only? Or pick a time period, like Shakespearian plays or early musicals.

To make the subject relevant to readers, you might relate your presentation to the present day. What tips can you offer current theater students from these long-ago performers?

Or you might focus primarily on costumes, set designs, or lighting. Those play a huge role in successful live theater.

I once asked a consultant—who works in several industries—if there was a secret to success. "The secret," he said, "is to provide a vital service that requires such specialization or expertise that nobody wants to compete with you."

As we have discussed earlier, single professional focus helps make people more successful. And because of that, some of them became famous.

Single-theme focus in a speech or report is what separates the great ones from the good ones. Lots of well-meaning speakers try to present several themes in a single speech, yet research says that listeners generally remember only two or three points.

There are many, many better speechwriters than I, and several terrific books on speaking. The only tip I can offer here:

The best speeches I've heard contain a single memorable line that listeners remember. Examples: Martin Luther King's "I have a dream" speech, or Franklin Roosevelt's inaugural address ("The only thing we have to fear is fear itself.").

You may not want to be a single-subject specialist, but you can master the skill that made them famous. Whenever you write a theme, report, or speech, try to focus on one major point.

Does Your Specialty Fit into Several Categories?

About 20 years ago I was sitting in the press room at a national business event when a famous comedian came in. He was headlining the program that evening, and asked if he could use the phone.

In the next 20 minutes—while I pretended not to listen—the comedian pulled out his planning calendar and booked himself at several other events in that area.

For him, name recognition was the key. When a radio or TV station knew he was in the region, they gladly scheduled him.

The veteran comedian knew that frequent, positive media exposure leads to even more invitations, more opportunities, and more income.

The successful multi-talent performer can appear in several media at once. The remarkable Will Rogers did this. He wrote a newspaper column, starred in a radio show, made movies, and appeared often on stage.

Even earlier, Mark Twain realized that his personal appearances enhanced his reputation as a master humorist and author.

And even before that, novelist Charles Dickens not only wrote novels and went on speaking tours but serialized some of his work in popular printed periodicals.

The Ideal Niche Business Model

Let me tell you about a long-time friend who built a near-perfect business. John's father was a 1950s era efficiency expert who served as consultant to manufacturing companies.

John—who held both a B.S. and M.B.A. in business, plus masters' and Ph.D. in psychology—joined his father's company and added a specialty: helping companies place the right managers in executive positions.

John's group was small and staffed with two or three consulting psychologists. They developed several psychological tests that searched for specific traits, like vocabulary, intuitive math skills, aggressiveness, motivation, empathy, and intelligence.

All the company's advertising came from word-of-mouth. The company constantly received referrals. Then one day, John was approached by a professional association.

The association asked if John could test several companies within a single profession. His job was to try to find a certain personality type of person who'd be successful in that field.

Before John died—far too young—he was helping entire industries find the right specialists to fill good-paying jobs.

At that point, he became a speaker at trade association conventions. He was in demand as a consultant every place he went.

John started out as a specialist. Then his clients helped him pioneer an incredible micro-niche.

Secret 17

Gather Information on Flash Fiction Techniques

At workshops I constantly tell attendees to read flash fiction (short stories under 1000 words). Don't read just one story. Read lots of them. Short biographies and short fiction require much the same format.

Good flash fiction has a rhythm and pace that's suitable for all types of short writing.

More important, it's nearly always about setting, a single character, mood, and simplicity.

But strive to write simple stories! One editor used to reject my stories with this phrase. "This is a nice feature, but I don't understand it. Remember, I am in sixth grade."

This hint reminded me that the average American reads at the seventh to eighth grade level, according to The Literacy Project. If you're unsure about your current writing, do a copy-and-paste test. Copy a few paragraphs, and paste them in at this link:

https://readabilityformulas.com/gunning-fog-readability-formula.php

One Minute Commercials: the Best Teacher?

A Simple Scene style—focusing on a single event and its implications—is the easiest way to present almost any concept.

Whenever I construct one, I think of the TV commercials I watch all the time. Most of my favorites are one minute. (Is that my short attention span?)

Sometimes, I watch a few of them to remind me to spotlight one problem and one solution. Anything more might complicate the message.

Why do most of us buy stuff? To solve a problem.

And the major question we answer in most stories is WHY. Why do I need a new mattress? Why is your mattress better than the one I already use? Why should I compare mattresses before I buy one?

The average oral reading speed is about 135-150 words per minute. Once you are finished writing, read your work aloud. It should take you two minutes or less.

Remember my personal rhythm-and-pacing method: I use no more than three sentences per paragraph.

Secret 18

Prepare to Create the Perfect Title or Heading

Suppose you pick up the paper tomorrow and see this headline: "Police begin campaign to run down jaywalkers."

Heck, I'll scan this story just to see if they've run over any of my friends! But wait, maybe the article means something else. Ah, yes, perhaps the police just want to ticket these folks.

But guess what? I'm already into the story. Like a giant vacuum, that weird headline sucked me right into the first paragraph.

Because, like a vacuum, I'm looking for dirt! OK, maybe not dirt. But for gossip, or strange news, or stuff nobody else knows.

Following are some more wild headlines. (I believe they're real. Many were sent to me by e-mail.) If you saw these unusual nuggets, would you read the story that followed?

Panda mating fails; veterinarian takes over

Dealers will hear car talk at noon

If strike isn't settled quickly, it may last awhile

Cold wave linked to temperatures

Two sisters reunite after 18 years at checkout counter

Headline sources: various papers, www.slinkycity.com

What's Wrong?

Did you notice something else about these titles? All of them are slightly incongruous. They just don't quite make sense. That's what forces us to read more.

Which heading would make you read more? "John Player wins game with touchdown" or "John Player's diving catch clinches playoffs."

Road Signs, Stop Signs, and Headlines

Picture yourself cruising down the highway. Left and right, huge signboards appear, then vanish as you drive past them. Occasionally, one or two catch your eye. Do you remember any of them?

Experts tell us these signs should be ten words or less. Otherwise, they could be both confusing and a traffic hazard.

Ask people who drove cars in the 1940s, '50s, and '60s which road signs they recall best. Most likely they'll say Burma Shave.

This shaving cream company created a series of messages that dotted the highways all over America. Each complete message required five or six small signs to reveal part of the story.

Each sign held only four or five words. The last sign revealed the sponsor: Burma Shave.

When writing your headline, think about Burma Shave's method. Catch the reader's attention but reveal only part of the message. Save the rest of the details for the story.

Another way to look at titles: the "Stop" sign perspective. We see hundreds of signs every day, but when we see the familiar red, six-sided stop sign, we do what we're told.

Your headline should do this too—force the reader to stop and look before going further.

51 Ways to Showcase Your Story with a Headline

1. Begin with the words who, what, when, where, why, or how. Who really won in "Three Little Pigs" story? Or, How to keep your home safe from windy wolves

2. Offer a test. Do you have these problems? or Do you have symptoms of _____?

3. Make a rhyme. Three pigs frolic and play after wolf runs away

4. The long list. Ten ways to improve your golf or Thirteen ways to find out if…

5. How to. How to captivate readers with your first few words

6. Real reason. The real reason two houses blew down

7. Don't do this. If you want a safer house, don't do this

8. Big problem. How Pig # 3 solved his chimney problem

9. Straight talk. The straight scoop on tasty ice cream

10. Accidental discovery. Accidental discovery of ancient pottery leads scientists to historic site.

11. What if. What if your house blew down tomorrow?

12. New help. New help for dry skin

13. Savings. Part-time student saves two hours a day

14. Rapid learning. Pig learns to build safe house in 12 days

15. Startling fact. Pig reveals startling facts about wolf's lung capacity

16. Opposites. Pig learns good lesson from bad experience

17. At last. After 100 years, new study of "Three Pigs" reveals author at last

18. Percentage or fraction. Two out of three readers believe fairy tales are true

19. Shock or outrage. Townspeople shocked by "Three Pigs" story

20. Fault or blame. Judge says wolf attack not pigs' fault

21. Strange or odd. Strange sounds leave citizens worried

22. Quick fix. Two-minute test offers amazing results

23. Categories or types. Researcher asks, "Which type are you?"

24. Prognostication. Broker predicts better stock market by next week

25. Inside secrets or tips. Escape secrets revealed by pigs

26. Open letter. Pigs send open letter to wolf community

27. Pass this test. Could you pass this fitness challenge?

28. What's wrong. What's wrong with this story?

29. Simplicity. Body builder tells simple method to keep fit

30. Ought to know or must know. What you must know about chimneys

31. Specific day, date, or time. July 4 means parades, celebrations in our town

32. Problem question. Fallen arches? Here's one overlooked reason

33. Imagine. What will life be like in 2050?

34. Nostalgia. Local citizen recalls days before cars

35. Breakthrough. Social worker announces breakthrough research on homelessness

36. Start from scratch. How local mosquito repellent company started from scratch

37. Mistake. The mistake that cost one teen a scholarship

38. Time pressure. Quick study methods revealed for students short on time

39. Right and wrong. Right and wrong ways to drive discussed

40. The unexpected. New aging research contradicts last year's results

41. Before and after. Pigs view wolves differently after break-ins

42. News from experts. Advice to nervous people from relaxation expert

43. Wild, crazy luck. Local waiter finds 1997 lottery ticket worth thousands

44. Long struggle, late success. After 30-year struggle, man denied schooling now reads well

45. Building momentum. Playoff foes share history of hard-fought competition

46. Privileged lifestyle. Jet-set weekends common for movie star

47. The dating game. Dating etiquette for the 21st century

48. Battle of the sexes. Number 1 reason men won't ask for directions

49. Setting a standard. Local umpire sets high standards for fair play and sportsmanship

50. Crazy mix-up. Error on application form creates hopeless confusion for woman during interview

51. The moral. Pennies really do make dollars, says local coin collector

As you scan this list, think about all the ways these headers could be altered slightly to fit your idea or product. And remember that the best headings often ask a question that can be answered by the story, prompt the reader to beg, "Tell me more," appeal to the reader's current needs, and, most importantly, offer new information.

Secret 19

Your First Sentence Is the Most Important One

Copywriting experts insist the headline's main purpose is to make the reader read the first sentence. The first sentence should be so good it sticks to the reader's mind like duct tape.

Why Getting those First Words Just Right Matters

Pretend for a moment you're a talent scout sitting in a small room. At 9 a.m. the door opens, and 100 entertainers race in. All begin their acts simultaneously. Some sing, a few dance, one juggles, another walks on her hands, still another one swings from the overhead light. What a madhouse.

Your readers face similar distractions. Of all the reports or stories available to them, how do they decide which ones to read?

What information is critical?

In some corporations, managers are given details on a need-to-know basis. They're provided data only if it relates directly to their areas of responsibility.

We writers should follow this rule. But often we don't. In sharing new information with a reader, we often provide too much history and background the reader doesn't need to know. All this superfluous junk bores the reader before she can get excited about our real story.

My Personal Favorite Story Openers

I admit that I am a lazy guy. I write a lot of memoirs, and I use the same formulas most of the time.

On the wall next to my desktop computer, I keep these eight powerful starting ideas. When I'm struggling for a way to get going, I just consult my small, wrinkled, coffee stained (I'm a slob) piece of paper, and it leads me forward.

Yes, for the last 30 years or so, I've been using these openers. They work for me nearly every time.

But if you don't like them, don't use them. In the next chapter you'll find 60 other approaches.

1. ASK A QUESTION -- How do you feel when somebody yells at you?'

2. START WITH DIALOG -- "Sarah, those leaves to your left are poison ivy!"

3. SECRET -- Yep, this word is magic. And I'm sharing secrets with you right now. I consider secrets valuable. Example: "The 1880s book we discovered revealed secrets of the Wild West."

4. FLASHBACK -- As we drove past the school, my mind took me back to my first day there.

5. HINT ABOUT FUTURE ACTION -- Our opponents across the field looked bigger, stronger, and older

6. CREATE A VIVID SCENE -- It's midnight, the car won't start, and I'm hopelessly lost.

7. WHAT IF -- What if you sat down to take a semester exam, and your mind suddenly went blank?

8. QUOTE that relates to the theme of your memoir -- Consult a directory of quotations for the most appropriate one.

Secret 20

You Don't Like My Favorite Sentences? Then Try These!

To see how other writers start a story, surround yourself with newspapers and magazines. Don't look for straight news (the who, what, where, when, why, and how stories).

Instead, you want to emulate features or editorials. Gather 15 or 20 features with particularly well-written first sentences.

What do they have in common? When I tried this, here's what I found.

1. Repeat the headline using different words. If the original headline says "Local citizen welcomes space aliens" your first sentence might proclaim "The local sheriff says space visitors are welcome at his home"

2. Suggest an alternative. For folks who don't have the time or inclination to devote two hours daily to studying the stock market, here's a possible alternative.

3. Set a scene. Researchers gathered in a packed laboratory today to hear results of the latest study on the common cold.

4. Present new evidence. Experts have spent years telling us exercise helps. But new evidence suggests you can get too much of a good thing.

5. Offer new hope. For aging baby boomers, there's new hope for a vaccine that slows aging in lab rats.

6. Ask why. Why do you always remember where you left the keys, but never remember where you left the car?

7. Reveal a discovery. While biking through the woods last month, I made a discovery that changed my life.

8. Recall a certain day. "On March 10, 1876, Alexander Graham Bell spoke into his phone, 'Mr. Watson, come here, I want to see you.'"

9. Relate an unforgettable event. I'll never forget the day I met my wife. Alternatively, often used in speeches: I'll always remember…

10. Predict or tell of a premonition. Little did I know when I entered that room what I was about to discover.

11. Use fear or horror. "The dog's missing," Dad said, and I froze in my tracks.

12. Reveal the magic keys. A high school baseball coach has developed five keys to a perfect swing.

13. Examine a ritual. For 50 years, former grads have returned to the old abandoned high school building at Homecoming to share memories of their school days.

14. Offer a checklist. Don't leave the office before trying these five techniques designed to help you work more efficiently.

15. Share a shortcut. Here's a method to race through a book, absorb the main points, and cut your reading time by half.

16. Emphasize ease. Here are three easy ways to check your carpet for mildew.

17. Explain cause and effect. If you've got a foot problem, it could be from one of these stress-related activities.

18. Describe a problem and its solution. Bob used to have trouble understanding conversations in a crowded room. Now, he's found a method to hear better.

19. Induce action by a time constraint. If you have these symptoms of lung disease, contact your doctor soon.

20. Disprove an old saying. Whoever said "You can't see the forest for the trees" must have looked in the wrong direction.

21. Give free advice. Free advice for the new father is as near as a computer web site.

22. Differ from the norm. Looking at the tall, slim Texan, you'd never guess he played defensive tackle in high school.

23. Contrast. John expected to feel much worse following the knee replacement, but thanks to modern techniques and these exercises, he improved quickly.

24. What would you do? Suppose you found yourself stuck on a dark country road late at night with no cell phone? What would you do?

25. Gaze upon the private person. Senator Statesman moves confidently through the crowd, smiling and shaking hands. Few know the shy youth inside, who struggled against many obstacles to reach his present position.

26. Stress the unbelievable. Outsiders can't believe the conditions in this city's schools. Experts say these crumbling structures need immediate attention.

27. Make immediate with the present tense. Larry smiles to himself as he jogs up the mountain. Every day he finds new scenery here.

28. Number the content. Next time you're hungry, try one of these ten proven one-minute recipes.

29. How I started. My first acting job paid nothing. It was a second-grade school play.

30. Where are they now? David Sportsman rarely comes to the ballpark anymore, because his new job gives him even more satisfaction than hitting home runs.

31. Consider the average. The average person travels 3.4 miles on foot during the day, but...

32. Display history repeating itself. The student walk-out yesterday seemed a radical move to new teachers, but not to veteran educators who recalled October of 1969.

33. Something's not right. Last week, when Joe searched his car for the contracts, he worried when he found them under his briefcase, not in the passenger seat where he left them.

34. Trivia. Here's information on the new football stadium for trivia buffs.

35. Surprises. If you always considered this town boring, wait until you hear about the surprises found in a 1933 time capsule unearthed at city hall last week.

36. Which did you choose? (This could also be called "Take this test.") What type are you? Answer the following 15 questions to find out if you're an introvert or an extrovert.

37. Word from the expert. Weather watcher Bob Maelstrom has correctly predicted the temperature on Thanksgiving for 30 years. What does he prognosticate this November?

38. Convincing evidence. Recent voter pattern studies offer convincing evidence that the incumbent mayor will win reelection.

39. Great idea. Susan Bee, a junior at the high school, revealed a new homecoming plan both students and teachers applaud.

40. Don't let this happen. Failure to check for a spare tire left one councilman miles away from a critical meeting last week.

41. Good news or alleviation of worry. Citizens who worried that the zoo might be closed can now breathe easier. An anonymous citizen has agreed to donate funds to pay for the needed repairs.

42. Best lesson learned. The college's football coach claims the most valuable lesson he learned came not on the field, but in an English class.

43. Working together. Last year this town endured a devastating flood. What steps can we take to prevent it this year?

44. Against the odds. On crutches since early September, quarterback Tom Touchdown saw little hope he'd be leading his team in October.

45. Road to success. This year's valedictorian says he followed a five-step daily study method, which he shared with reporters who covered the graduation ceremony.

46. Dream comes true. How many of us aspire to be a state champion of anything? When Lisa Jogger began training for cross-country running, she never imagined how far she'd travel.

47. Now hear this. A national committee on aging unanimously reported that the following 15 suggestions might make everyone healthier.

48. Guessing game. Can you guess the three topics people worry about most often?

49. The legend. Legendary radio announcer Mark Microphone addressed 10,000 fans at the convention center last night and offered tips for anyone wanting to present a message more clearly and effectively.

50. Shared traits. What traits do we share with insects, and how have they helped us survive thousands of years?

51. Shifting gears/radical departure. Movie idol David Film shifts personalities completely for his next starring role.

52. The new category. Pop singer Tiffany Audio exemplifies a whole group of young performers who share several unique traits.

53. Is she alive? Former 1940s starlet Jean Screen appeared in town last week for the first time in 60 years. Or did she?

54. Unexpected occurrence. Who'd expect an 83-year-old, who started exercising only five years ago, to take first place in 2021's citywide one-mile walk?

55. Uncanny ability. High school scholar Mark Algebra claims his consistently high classroom scores are based on his skill at recalling, almost word-for-word, lectures by his teachers.

56. What do you really know? Most townspeople know Main Street can pose major traffic hazards, but what do we really know statistically about accident frequency there?

57. Like mother like daughter. Twenty-five years ago, Sheila Smart took first place in the town spelling bee. This year, her daughter Lisa returned the title to the family.

58. Ever think about this? Do you ever think about life on other planets? Many experts say it exists, but it's different from ours.

59. Strange but true. A new research technique claims 79% effectiveness in predicting future events.

60. Reunions. After 40 years living separate lives, twin brothers reunited here last week, and found they had much in common.

The Secret of First Paragraphs

The power of the first sentence or two is simply this: It makes every reader ask, "What happens next?" or say "Really? Tell me more." It briefly explains what the rest of the article is all about. If the first paragraph does not convincingly lead to the next paragraph, it should be rewritten.

Now you've got 68 ways to begin each Simple Scene.

Secret 21

What's the Best Way to Conclude a Simple Scene?

I've always thought ending a story was like leaving a party. If I just grab my coat and walk out the door, people might wonder what happened. Was I upset? Was there an emergency?

Therefore, I must first prepare to leave by excusing myself from the conversation, thanking the hosts, and telling my friends goodbye. My exit, then, is part of a natural progression.

Likewise, ending a report or theme should sound natural to the reader. If you begin the ending well, readers will expect the conclusion in the next few sentences.

Here are 30 ways to say goodbye, yet make the reader wish you'd stay. Oh yes, I've brought those three little piggies back into a few examples. Is this what they call pigging out?

1. Headline reference. (Suppose your headline, or title, reinforces the value of planning.) The three little pigs remind us that we can hope for the best, but we must prepare for the worst.

2. Quote that restates the conclusion you've previously drawn. No doubt Edgar Watson Howe was thinking of Pig #1 and Pig #2 when he said, "A good scare is worth more to a man than good advice."

3. Discover. The three pigs discovered that cutting corners and lack of preparation can be keys to disaster.

4. Remember. The pigs will always remember the two lessons they learned from the mean wolf...

5. Success secrets. The three pigs remind us that one secret to success is...

6. Checklist. Next time you find yourself in a dangerous predicament like our little pig friends, think about these three escape routes.

7. Time constraint. This story reminds us that home security systems can begin to protect now and warn against any wolves who come knocking tomorrow.

8. Reinforce old saying. That old saying "Here today, gone tomorrow" certainly describes the first two pigs' houses.

9. Advice. Follow the advice of Pig # 3, who told his brothers...

10. Failed expectations. The first two pigs never expected to find themselves homeless. They really needed homeowners' insurance.

11. Numbering. The pigs learned five things from their experience with the mean wolf.

12. History lesson. The pigs won't forget that day the wolf left them homeless, nor will they let this history repeat itself.

13. Expert's advice. David Lumber, an experienced builder, says he'd offer the pigs three reminders on future construction.

14. Powerful evidence. The pigs' experience offers convincing evidence that...

15. Don't let this happen. Don't let what happened to the three pigs happen to you.

16. Shared traits. Sometimes we humans, in an effort to save money and time, take the same path as the first two pigs.

17. Inspirational thought. In today's tough world, with wolves around every corner, it's nice to know that most of us still look after others.

18. Writer's message. I think about those three little pigs all the time, and how they supported each other. We'd do well to follow their example.

19. Which one are you? How do your classmates see you? As the friend who'll protect them from pain, or the wolf who tries to take advantage of each situation?

20. Complete change. Their brush with danger changed these three brothers from helpless piglets to independent hogs.

21. What are the odds? This story reminds us that 66% of homeowners don't carry enough insurance.

22. Need more information? Ever wonder if during hard times you could keep the wolf from your door? For an informative brochure, just call 000-000-0000.

23. The facts are obvious. We all know we must be prepared for the worst. We hear horror stories every day about unlocked homes. But what can we do about it today?

24. Facts disprove theory. So, despite the views of a few skeptics, Pig #3's actions prove that hogs can reason.

25. Do me a favor. If you believe as I do that pigs make good pets, write your congressman today and ask him to sponsor the Pork Barrel bill.

26. Restated saying. The pigs' well-fortified brick home not only kept the wolf away from the door, but discouraged his entry from the chimney, too.

27. Want to read more? For Three Pigs fans, two other excellent titles on the pig-and-wolf battles are...

28. Luck or skill? After all these years, readers can't decide. Did pure luck or good planning eventually save the pigs?

29. Hidden meaning. Sure, we can all learn a lesson about safety from the pigs. But the story's hidden meaning is this: A wolf who doesn't work out can't expect unlimited lung power when he needs it most.

30. Topping a joke. Sadly, the pigs discovered that the wolf's bark was worse than his bite, but his breath was the worst of all.

Secret 22
Additional Uses for the Simple Scene

There are many ways to write about someone's experiences. Let's review those forms one more time:

The biography is the story of a person's life, often presented in chronological form, from beginning to end. An autobiography is a story of a person's life, written by that person herself or himself.

My specialty – the memoir -- is a group of memories, written as a first-person account by that person. It might be presented chronologically, or as a series of unrelated events that shaped that person's thinking.

An obituary usually begins with the announcement of a person's death, and it ends with a list of family members and friends important to the deceased's life. The middle paragraphs provide highlights of that person's life experience (education, career, civic activities, etc.).

<u>An Episodic Autobiography Can be Written as a Memoir</u>

Here's a technique that's over 100 years old. I've seen it many times.

Some experts claim that Mark Twain developed this approach for his own biography.

Instead of moving chronologically from one pivotal event to another, Twain brilliantly talked about his life's most exciting episodes. To paraphrase this master storyteller, when he began to get bored with an episode, he simply moved on.

What a great concept! If your current story or feature concerns you, you might begin your treasure hunt for your own best stories this way:

1. Talk to your family, friends, and clients. What stories do they remember about you? What specific ways might people say you helped them?

2. Meet with your former teachers. What skills and traits do they recall about you when you were a child?

3. Think about national events that have happened since you've been born. How did those events impact your life? For instance, Mark Twain talked about being born when Haley's Comet could be seen. (It's visible from earth once every 75-76 years.)

Episodic Biography Can Conclude With a Message

Aesop did it. So did Aristophanes and Mark Twain. You can do it too.

Memorable articles focus on individuals. Readers like to know about how others solve problems, and how they develop dreams and ideas.

Storytelling originated with prehistoric humans, who needed something to do while eating around the campfire. (There weren't many televisions back then.)

During the Middle Ages storytellers traveled a circuit, moving from castle to castle along with magicians, minstrels, and other entertainers.

There's always a great demand for storytellers. There still is. Look at the huge number of dramas and sitcoms on TV which require new episodes every week.

Would you like to attempt episodic writing before attempting your own memoir? Then select a long-deceased famous person. Jot down five or six things she accomplished during her life. Then, turn the information into a story – or a series of stories -- of 150-300 words that spotlights only one of those accomplishments.

The Easiest Way to Write Any Biography: Question-Answer Interview

On a few occasions, I've been asked to write a short memoir or biography that's scheduled to be published in the next few days.

That's scary, because even for a 300-500 word biography, it takes a little time to do the research. So—just in case you're faced with this—here's a simple idea:

Write that biography as a personal, question-answer interview. Talk to the subject, take careful interview notes so you quote the person exactly, and…you've got it!

In these situations, I always let the person I interview look over my story, to make sure I've captured her answers correctly.

The key components of the story still remain constant. I also think it's important that the interviewee describe the twist, or the pivotal point in his life when he decided to pursue the specialty you're writing about.

Secret 23
More Types of Simple Scenes

A Business-Marketing Simple Scene

Luke worried often about his toy store, one of three in the region. Its full inventory included dolls, board games, action figures and more.

When he checked store sales records, he discovered one customer who bought lots of HO scale model train cars. That customer also bought miniature houses and trees to build train "villages." This gave Luke an idea.

Quickly, Luke ordered more cars and trucks for those train sets... and tiny toy people to populate that miniature village. What happened?

Well, that customer sung the praises of Luke's store to other train hobbyists. The downsized products sold like crazy, and soon Luke eliminated his slower-selling inventory. The next year he spotlighted only miniature items.

The store filled with little train cars, 2" tall trees, miniature houses, tiny doll furniture, small action figures, and so on. People came from miles around to ask Luke's advice on building their own "miniature cities."

Luke didn't stop there. He began to speak throughout the region on constructing "a room-size city" in available space.

Luke had literally built his inventory by shrinking it!

A Path-to-Success Simple Scene

Readers love stories about "making lemonade out of lemons." This is also used frequently in "how-to" books.

Here's a small tale about how one particular service could be offered as a special skill.

My mother's father died before I was born. One day I asked my dad about him.

"Before he passed away," Dad remembered, "he'd built a good real estate clientele. He sold lots of houses because he wanted to tell prospective shoppers what was wrong with each residence.

"Old Tom had an eye for detail. When a house came on the market, he got there early and went over it with a fine-tooth comb. No imperfection escaped his eye, and he wrote down whatever he saw.

"When a prospective buyer asked his opinion on a property, Tom pulled out his flaw sheet. At a glance, the prospect could see everything that was wrong."

Strangely, prospects might begin to defend this problem property! Wait a minute, they might think. For only a few thousand bucks, this house could be a showplace.

Tom's honesty and eye for errors won him new customers. It also resulted in fewer complaints after the sale.

Because I am a biographer, I talk to other interviewers constantly. "What," I ask them, "is the one thing you most want to learn in an interview?"

Several told me this. "First, I want the person to tell me what they do best. Then, I want to know what they'd like to share with my readers."

Specialty, plus a secret. What does a person do, and why do they do it well?

To me, that's the skeleton—the foundation—to every biography.

I worked for one editor who told me that the how and why were the key components to any feature story. HOW did a person become prominent at her/his specialty, and WHY should the reader care?

Create-Your-Own-Specialty Simple Scene

Below is another sample Simple Scene. This story emphasizes the man's role as a "professional sports mascot."

How many experienced sports mascots do you know?

Jerry Sportsman qualifies. He wore a tiger costume in middle school, a skunk disguise in high school, and now represents his college as an eagle. How did he get started?

"I was a terrible athlete," Jerry laughs. "I got picked last for every sports team. The team who selected me just had to put me in a position where I'd do the least harm."

But a freakish event in middle school put Jerry on the road to sports fame. "My best friend was our middle school mascot, and he twisted his knee during halftime at our first football game. We were the same size, so I put on his uniform at halftime."

No one recognized Jerry, and the anonymous tiger stalked the sidelines, cheering his team to victory.

"My friend would take five weeks to recover, so the principal said I could be mascot in the next game too." During that week, Jerry studied films of actual tigers, and learned to imitate their moves.

"In high school," Jerry remembers, "I competed for the skunk job. But I had a secret plan.

"I wore my little costume. But right before I competed, I sprayed myself with great cologne.

"I think they chose me because I looked bad, but I smelled really good."

Secret 24

Use the Simple Scenes Approach for Personal Interviews

I've often been hired by magazines and newspapers to create "profiles" about prominent people or businesses in a community.

It's important to get answers to all major questions. But it's even more important to create questions that help the interviewee tell a complete, compelling story. How does one do this?

In earlier chapters, we've talked about discovering the "twist" in a story. When I interview someone, I'm looking for something slightly different.

Different Interview Styles

My radio friend Dave laughs about the day he interviewed the mayor of a large town. "How much time before your show starts?" the mayor asked.

When Dave told him two minutes, the mayor asked, "Do you think I've got enough time to go comb my hair?" I guess the mayor didn't notice that radio doesn't require cameras.

Dave's story reminds me that while style requirements in radio and TV vary, it takes a special person to conduct a mesmerizing interview. The interviewer profession grows as the number of interactive mediums (e-mail, telephone, social media, etc.) expands.

Many good public interactors are radio talk show hosts. This job is very hard, because hosts must be agile enough to keep an interview lively, reactive enough to respond to guests' answers with more questions, and verbose enough to fill silent airtime if a talk show guest clams up.

I've spent most of my working life as a print interviewer, not an on-air one. I can take my time getting to know the person I interview.

After several preliminary questions like "Where were you born?" and "What do you remember from your early school days?" I can move forward to more important queries.

But a radio or television host must move faster. They must get to the heart of a subject quickly, and they must do it in a way the keeps the audience engaged.

A Step-by-Step Interview Approach

1. Let's say I'm interviewing a coach. I'll call him Kevin. The first several questions are simply to relax Kevin. I'll ask him his full name, why that name was given to him, where and when he was born, and if he had siblings.

2. Next, I'll ask about early schooling. What were elementary and high schools like?

3. Then, I'll ask about his profession. When did Kevin meet his first coach, and in what sport?

Was there a particular coach he admired? What did Kevin learn from that person?

4. If I don't get a satisfactory response to a question, I'll try phrasing it another way.

5. I start moving toward the "twist" question. In this case, the question would be, "Do you remember the moment you decided you would become a coach?"

6. The twist question is a little like asking a couple, "What moment did you first realize you were in love?" The couple will likely give you two different answers. (I know...I've tried this!)

7. The twist should never be used in a negative way. It will likely be the "turning point" in a biography. If our hypothetical coach here – Kevin -- can tell me the exact moment he decided to coach, I can then help him flesh out the rest of his timeline, up to the present day.

If he recalls no specific event, I will ask how-or-why questions to help him determine a time range when he selected coaching. That event or time range then becomes the high point of the interview.

8. On some occasions, I will get nothing! It is a horrible interview. That's when I start looking around the room, using my "sight-and-write" technique. I notice random objects to ask questions about.

Example: "I see several books on your desk. Have any books changed your life? What's your favorite book?"

9. What's the ideal question to ask to end his interview? I think it's one of these: "What are your plans for the future? What do you want your players to remember most about you?"

Secret 25

How a Simple Scene Tackles School Essays and Reports

Writing high school and college essays is a pain. How many have you written? Are you a student who writes essays all the time?

My approach is (a) look at the topic of the essay, and (b) decide how many questions a reader would expect the essay to answer.

Let's tackle two common essay types. The first is the college application essay, and the second is the generic high school term theme or essay requirement.

College Application Essay

In our state, students can construct essays from three prompts. They're required to write between 350 and 650 words. The first two prompts are biographical.

A: What unique opportunities or challenges have you experienced throughout your high school career that have shaped who you are today?

B: Some students have an identity, or interest, or a talent that defines them in an essential way. If you are one of these students, tell us about yourself.

C: You've got a ticket in your hand. Where will you go? What will you do? What will happen when you get there?

Essays A and B can be written in the first person. When you consider A, ask yourself: "Will 'my opportunity' or 'my challenge' make a more unusual story?"

If you choose Essay B, you might explain how you discovered your special talent. (Here's an example of Essay A. Pay attention to the story's twist.)

It was just another boring day in drama class when it happened.

Our textbook contained a bunch of short, one-act plays. The teacher chose one, and she assigned us parts. Five of us gathered at the front of the room.

I played the part of an old man. I lowered my voice the best a 15-year-old can, and then I read my lines.

But I had a special gift in my throat that day: a head cold. It lowered my voice another octave.

After class, the teacher called me to her desk. "Charlie," she said, "I have never heard that voice before. I'd like for you to meet a friend of mine at the radio station who hires speaking voices for commercials." (Twist)

That's how my high school career as a part-time announcer began...Etc.

Essay C invites students to write a fictional account. The best one I've seen was submitted by a Texas student who talked about winning a two-week European vacation, and her adventures there.

In her essay, this lady researched a country and its history, which included historical sites. Her twist came near the end of the essay, where she met a guy who became a short-time boyfriend and later a pen pal.

Basic School Essays, Themes, or Book Reports

Many school essays require either a brief biography, synopsis of a historical event, or a book report.

If you're writing a biography or explaining a historical event, it helps to create the story line we discussed earlier. (That's a single sentence summation that gives the main goal of the story.)

Then, you can decide to build it chronologically, or if you should construct it around a pivotal event.

I begin by writing a story line for the essay, detailing in a single sentence what I want the reader to learn.

Then, I develop a series of questions that will take the reader through the story in a logical way.

In the following example, I'm writing about a major league baseball player, and how he developed a special skill. So, I'll write myself some questions to answer that would lead the reader to better understand:

(1) When did Sam start playing baseball? (2) What made him decide he had a special athletic gift? (3) How did Sam discover a way to differentiate himself from other players on the team? Etc.

I then follow up with a twist line spotlighting the turning point in my story. (Once again, I repeat: a fantastic twist line can make all the difference!)

That twist line might look something like this:

Major leaguer Tom _____ was an average minor league player before discovering the special gift that makes him a major leaguer today. (Story line)

Tom developed a short-swing batting technique during spring training while recovering from shoulder surgery. (Twist)

In school, I wrote dozens of book reports. I hated the process. However, by using the Simple Scene technique – asking myself questions I'd need to answer to help enlighten the reader -- I learned to quickly spotlight the high points of any book, then conclude with a short summation. Here's how the classic story *Charlotte's Web* might be reviewed.

(As usual, I'll indicate where I put the twist, or turning point of the story.)

Wilber the pig is in a tough spot. Farmer Zuckerman is raising him for meat. How can he escape this fate?

Wilbur's spider friend Charlotte has a plan. Using her web-making skills, she starts weaving wonderful phrases about Wilbur in the barn.

The barn suddenly becomes a local tourist attraction. (Twist) Folks come from all around to see Wilbur, and he's even honored at the local county fair.

Charlotte, by now an old spider, realizes that her life mission to save Wilbur has succeeded, and that Zuckerman will now keep and cherish Wilbur. Sadly, Charlotte dies while attending that fair.

Wilbur returns to the farm with some of Charlotte's spider eggs, and new little spiders emerge to keep Wilbur company.

Wilbur is eternally grateful to Charlotte. He realizes that real friends are those who look for -- and appreciate -- the good in those that they care about.

Secret 26

Simple Scenes for Speech Introductions and Reference Letters

In both these circumstances, you want the audience member or letter recipient to say, "Wow, I cannot wait to meet this outstanding person!"

As you'll recall from earlier in this book, we talked about how a "twist" takes a Simple Scene in a different direction.

For instance, if a talented young baseball player decides to become a pitcher and focuses his training there, that would be a mild twist in the story.

Or, that twist could be a total surprise the reader didn't expect. Example: In *The Wizard of Oz,* Dorothy and her friends suddenly discover that the Wizard is just an ordinary man.

Speech Introduction Technique

I once heard somebody say that a speech introduction should last no longer than two minutes. I think it should be shorter than that.

One of my pet peeves at some speaking events is that too many people are scheduled. A keynote address should be just that. The key speaker should be introduced with a flourish.

How many times have you heard the master of ceremonies come to the microphone, then introduce everyone on stage, and each one's spouse, then introduce the person who will introduce the guest speaker? Why, why, why?

The best intros I've heard do not say the name of the speaker until the last two words…the person's first and last names.

Until that moment, the speech Introduction should be a "tease," providing one enticing sentence after another until the name is announced.

Look at the introduction below and tell me if it makes you eager to hear what the speaker will say.

Speech Introduction Sample

How many of you carry a cell phone equipped with a camera? 100%, correct?

And how many of you would like to improve the quality of your pictures? How many of you wish you could take photos that are so good, you want to frame them?

We predict your life is about to change in the next 20 minutes. That's because our speaker is about to share some skills she's discovered in 30 years as a magazine photographer.

So, what would you like to do with your camera? Enhance colorful flower scenes? Capture the grandkids as they play games around the house? Take a meaningful snapshot of grandma and grandpa on their 60th anniversary?

You'll hear about that and much more...like how to capture moving images of sports events, or candid pictures of your dog fetching a ball.

We could tell you more, but we won't. Our speaker today is waiting to show you much more. So, help me say hello to our special visitor today, whose photos have graced the covers of over 200 magazines. Welcome, Phyllis Photo.

Reference Letter Technique

My first question is this: Will you be writing a letter first person—about yourself—or will you be recommending another person?

If you're writing about yourself, perhaps one of your first few sentences should talk about the special skill you want to tell your prospective employer about.

Therefore, you might begin with something like this:

I first discovered my art abilities in the third grade one day, when the teacher asked us to try to sketch a horse. In only a couple of minutes, I had something ready to show her.

The teacher looked amazed. "You have profound potential, Stephanie," she said. "I think you could be a professional artist."

From that time forward, I sought potential school and professional assignments. (Continue with your story.)

Reference Letter Sample for Someone Else

I've always thought the hardest part of a reference letter is keeping—and holding—the reader's attention.

I suggest using the declare-prepare method we discussed earlier. Limit each paragraph to three sentences or less, and make sure the last sentence entices the reader to read the next paragraph. So, the letter might begin something like this:

I want to introduce you to a young lady who grew up next door to me. I never realized how special she was until one day last summer, when her quick thinking and college training saved a life.

This special person, Debbie _____, graduated from nursing school last month. She has been working part-time in our hardware store while sending resumes to hospitals.

Last week, an older gentleman collapsed at our store. (Briefly tell the rest of the story.)

Secret 27

A Simple Scene for Obituaries, Tributes, and Funeral Speeches

The Simple Scene is a powerful way to build a moving eulogy or tribute. There are several sorts you may encounter. The obituary is more structured. Let's talk about that first.

An obituary might be read or saved for years, so it's important that we get the words just right. We want to honor the deceased, and we also want to provide a keepsake for family and friends.

I still have my grandparents' obituaries, and I will pass them along to my child and grandchildren.

Most families want the primary obituary to be in the town where the deceased lived. Some newspapers charge to run an obituary; some do not.

And some papers may charge different rates for long or short obituaries. Some may charge to include a photo.

Talk to the newspaper about price first. In my experience, there is usually no charge for an online obituary. I'm guessing many funeral homes offer free obituaries on their company web sites.

Upfront, most obituaries give the deceased's full name, date and place of birth and death, age, the next of kin or close family members, date-time-place of funeral, and where to send flowers, or where to make a donation. (Check your local paper for style.)

Also, depending on the newspaper, most obits follow a standard format, and rarely have a headline above the person's name.

Of course, if the deceased is famous or noteworthy, a headline often appears which describes the deceased's "claim to fame." If the paper allows longer obituaries—which sometimes happens in smaller newspapers—it might resemble a short news story.

To develop this obituary, I have asked myself to answer these questions:

How did Boomer die? What made his demise unusual? What feats did he accomplish? What did relatives say about him? Who are his survivors? What details on his memorial service will readers want to know?

Here's a sample (248 words). Note that in the last sentence of every paragraph, I "invite" the reader to keep reading by promising more details.

130-year-old athlete Dies During 100-Meter Dash

Babe E. Boomer passed away last week during an Ultra-Senior Track and Field Competition. Onlookers say he crossed the finish line just before he finished permanently. What was his longevity secret?

Boomer attended more schools than a class ring salesman, and earned so many degrees he ran out of wall space. The day after his untimely death, he was scheduled to begin classes in public speaking.

Like many others his age, Boomer plans to speak via a pre-recorded video at his own "celebration of life" at 10 AM January 17 in Anytown Church. "Dad didn't want some stranger to give his eulogy," said Boomer's son Babe, Jr. "Also, he wanted to say a lot of nice things about himself." Attendees anticipate surprises.

His rambling eulogy will offer comments about family and friends. But the highlight will be comments on what it means to be a Baby Boomer.

"In my youth we drank water from the garden hose, and thought it tasted fine. We didn't text message in class. And we always planned for the future."

Naturally, Boomer left instructions that his body be frozen immediately after his death, and thawed out if he could be revived. His large family supports that.

Survivors include his wife, 2.3 children (the statistically average number for a Baby Boomer), 17 grandchildren, too many great-grandchildren to count, an antique mid-1960's convertible with dual exhausts, and a variable rate mortgage he refinanced 11 times.

Memorial service: Thursday, April 7 at 2:30 PM, Cityside Cemetery Chapel. No flowers, please. Donations may be made to _____.

Tributes and Eulogies

When I write eulogies—and I've written several—I rarely talk about a person's death. Instead, I focus on the one or two traits that made her a special person.

To do that, I ask family members to describe the person. I want to know what she was especially proud of, and what she liked to talk about.

I want to know about early life, schooling, her relationship with parents, and activities she enjoyed with her children.

What sports did she like? What jokes did she tell? What would she like descendants to know? What things irritated or annoyed her?

Did she value private time, or parties, or going to sports events? Did she have a preferred pet or car? Did she want friends to contribute to a certain charity in his name?

Most important of all, what truly made her happy? And finally, what lessons can we—the living—learn from her life?

The Rule of Threes

This is an old writing concept I use for all my presentations, not just eulogies.

This method is also called a triad. It spotlights the power of three. For instance, you hear lots of these phrases in everyday life, including "stop, look, and listen" or patriotic concepts like "duty, honor, and country."

You've also read stories like *The Three Little Pigs,* or *The Three Musketeers,* or *Goldilocks and the Three Bears.*

How do you use that in a eulogy? I might begin the talk with something surprising like, "If Mary were here with us today…well, she would not be here today, because she hated funerals."

Following that gentle remark, I would share three brief stories that made Mary unique. And I would link each short story together with a connector sentence.

Eulogy Technique Example

Mary was always the fastest runner in our class. She never lost, and always said "Second place is fine, but first place is finer." (Tell the rest of this story.)

(Connector) Yes, running came naturally to Mary. We kidded her that she ran for every class office, and that she'd be perfectly happy to hold all senior class offices simultaneously. (Tell rest of story.)

(Connector) From high school president to college class officer. From college class officer to corporate officer. From corporate officer to non-profit officer, to a nationally known innovator for non-profit organizations. (Tell rest of story.)

(Conclusion) What Mary teaches us is that life is about running toward goals that help others. Every day, get up and get running. Run for your life, for the rest of your life.

Thank you, Mary, for your tenacity, energy, and compassion.

Bottom line: How long should a eulogy or funeral oration be? Twenty minutes at the most…but 15 minutes is better.

I once asked a well-known minister what his sermon would be about the following Sunday. He smiled and said, "It will be about 12 minutes."

Secret 28

Other Questions about Simple Scenes

I have interviewed hundreds of people, and many are intimidated if I ask them to tell about their lives. They immediately start a chronology, telling me where they were born, what elementary school they attended, and so on.

"No, no, no," I gently say. "I don't want to know about your timeline. I want to know about your major decisions.

What is the easiest way to start a Simple Scene memoir?

Think about all the big memories of your life. These can be good or bad. Then put that memory in the form of an interview question.

If the first thing you can remember is moving to a new apartment, ask yourself "Why did we move to a new apartment when I was two years old?"

Answer that question by writing down every memory you have of that event.

Conclude by describing what you learned from that occasion.

Tell me about the concept of "in medias res."

That's just the Latin words for "in the midst of things." A fiction writer – instead of starting at the beginning – would transport the reader to the middle of the story.

I love this idea, and I use it for nearly all the memoirs and biographies I write.

For instance, instead of starting a story about a sports trainer or exercise therapist, I drop him right into an action scene that changed his life.

Here's a sample:

I am playing third base. There's a runner on second, and he races toward me as the batter swings.

The grounder goes to the pitcher, who throws me the ball. I tag the runner, and I feel a sting in my hand. No pain, just a sting.

I pull off my glove, and my thumb looks disfigured. I suddenly remember the first time I needed an exercise therapist.

How would you describe a "story arc?"

I have understood it to be a detailed or extended chronological story plot line. This could be used for movies, stage shows, or even ongoing series.

I don't worry about this when writing Simple Scenes. I construct these as stand-alone events.

When I finish writing all of them, I re-read them and ask myself: Is there a recurring theme or "lesson learned" in all these unrelated events?

If so, that becomes the title for the group of questions the subject answered.

Do you have a "personal secret" for writing Simple Scenes?

Yes. And remember that I am always focused on about 300 words. I want every scene (or episode) I write to be this short.

Also, I nearly always include a "failure factor" in each story. Before the scene – or a person – succeeds, I present a potential failure or conflict. Example:

The geometry test was tomorrow morning, and Frank had a big problem. He failed last week's test, and if he failed again he would not graduate. Etc.

Should memoirs end on an upbeat or inspiring note?

I am a big believer in a resolved conclusion. Some writers don't agree.

I have heard story arcs described as an elevator…up and down, up and down.

I don't agree. I think memoirs should be positive progression upward. The main character keeps trying to improve himself and his life.

How can I make my answer read like a movie or stage scene?

Write down what happened to you informally...just like you were talking to a friend.

Don't make this complicated. Just describe a moment.

Your short reply should have a beginning and end. The end should be a conclusion of that episode. It's also helpful if it informs the reader about a discovery, or a lesson you learned.

How can I make my short episodes more readable?

Make sure you put your setting (scene or location) and problem in the first paragraph.

The problem can be virtually any fear. Examples: a villain, animal, disease, weather, social isolation, loneliness, depression.

It's easier for the reader if only two people are in each scene.

Talk about the obstacles you must overcome to solve the problem. Then tell how you solved it...or what happened to the problem. Did it go away, or appear later?

Is it harder to write about yourself, or another person?

It is much harder to write about someone else, because the writer does not know how that other person thinks.

However, if I am writing about a married couple – or a memoir of two long-time business partners – I have found it fairly easy to get my questions answered. And most of those memoirs have turned out well.

What other ideas can improve a Simple Scene?

You might explain complex concepts with a simile (a comparison using like or as) or a metaphor. Example: "A turtle shell is like a house the animal can carry on its back."

Another idea: When you finish each Simple Scene, read it out loud to hear how it sounds. If it sounds boring…rewrite it.

What's the hardest thing about writing Simple Scenes?

When most people are asked questions about themselves, they fall into a "chronology zone." That is, most want to provide a "back story" to explain why they chose a certain profession, or changed jobs during a certain year.

That does not improve a Scene. A scene's drama relies on the emotion expressed at the time a major decision is made.

Example: If I'm interviewing a famous historian, I do not care about how many times he changed his major during college. What I want to write about is the instant he decided to become a history professor, and what his thought process was at that time.

What makes the Simple Scene superior?

Not everyone can write a biography, novel, or short story. But we can all talk about our lives.

Secret 29

When You Are Ready to Start Typing...

Don't want to type? Then try this:

Find several questions from some of the memoir sites provided earlier. Or, create a list of your own questions.

Ask yourself each of these questions – then provide an answer, using an audio-to-Word-document like Google Docs Voice Typing, Dragon Naturally Speaking, or similar programs.

Should you employ a memoirist?

I nearly always recommend a memoirist for non-writers. I used one myself even though I write biographies for a living.

Memoirists can supply you good questions to build your episodes, typeset and design a book, and then print as many as you want.

The price range is flexible. You can spend as little as $100-$200. Or, you can ask a memoirist to interview you. (Price is around $1000 and up, plus printing the number of books you want.)

Use a memoirist to help you compose your book, then decide if you would like to hire a printer to publish copies you can offer to clients.

Short or long book?

To make your memoir shorter, just ask yourself fewer of the questions you make up yourself, or that the memoirist supplies you.

Some people feel a long memoir is too intimidating. Therefore – after you develop many questions -- select 25-50 favorite questions to answer.

Tell the memoir company when you've written everything you want to write.

That's when they will put your original manuscript together.

Who are some memoir companies?

There are several great memoir companies who ask questions that reawaken memories. And as mentioned earlier, you can add your own questions also.

Purchase oftentimes includes a log-in to the company's web site to begin answering questions, writing stories, and uploading photos.

Front covers can be fully and individually customized.

The book can be up to several hundred pages long. Additional hard copies and digital copies can be ordered. And, you may even want to choose an audiobook option.

For more details plus a discount, go to this site: Memorygram Memoir. You can use code rix20 at checkout for a discount. (This article contains affiliate links, which means writer may receive a commission on any sales of products or services described here.)

Finally…

I can personally teach you how to write Simple Scenes. You can e-mail at rix@rixquinn.com to schedule an appointment.

Once you begin using these techniques, I think you will want to start using them for all your writing.

I use Simple Scenes for virtually all my writing. It makes my professional life much simpler.

www.ingramcontent.com/pod-product-compliance
Lightning Source LLC
LaVergne TN
LVHW061038070526
838201LV00073B/5095